Face the Facts
Racism

Adrian Cooper

For information, address the publisher:
Raintree, 100 N. LaSalle, Suite 1200, Chicago, IL 60602

Design by Jamie Asher/Mayer Media
Printed and bound in China.
07 06 05 04 03
10 9 8 7 6 5 4 3 2 1

Library of Congress Cataloging-in-Publication Data

Cooper, Adrian.
  Racism / Adrian Cooper.
    v. cm. -- (Face the facts)
Contents: What is racism? -- Race and racists : what is race? -- Racism in history -- Racism in society -- Racism and you -- Experiences of racism -- Facts and figures.
  ISBN 0-7398-6434-3 (HC), 1-4109-0047-9 (Pbk.)
  1. Racism--Juvenile literature. [1. Racism.] I. Title. II. Series.
HT1521 .C636 2003
305.8--dc21
                           2002013050

Acknowledgments
The publishers would like to thank the following for permission to reproduce photographs:
pp. 1, 10, 12, 14, 17 AKG London; p. 5 (top), 37 David Hoffman Photo Library; p. 5 (bottom) Nick Cobbing/David Hoffman Photo Library; pp. 6–7, 32, 38, 39, 47, 48–49 Image Works/Topham Picturepoint; p. 7 Ancient Art and Architecture Collection; pp. 7, 15, 19 (top), 28 (top) Prosport/Topham Picturepoint; p. 9 Ronnie Kaufman/Corbis Stock Market; pp.16, 28 (bottom), Reuters/Popperfoto; p. 19 (bottom) Robert W. Kelly/Timepix/Rex Features; p. 21 Mirek Towski/Rex Features; p. 22 Camera Press; pp. 24, 25, 30 Nils Jorgensen/Rex Features; p. 27 Steve Chenn/Corbis; p. 31 Terry Thompson/Rex Features; p. 34 MXL/Rex Features; p. 36 Dita Alangkara/Associated Press; p. 36 Santiago Lyon/Associated Press; p. 41 PA/John Stillwell/Topham Picturepoint; p. 43 (top) Marcus Zeffler/Rex Features; p. 43 (bottom) Mike Hutchings/Reuters/Popperfoto; pp. 44–45 Richard Young/Rex Features; p. 50 John Birdsall Photography.

Cover photograph: Format/Ulrike Press

Every effort has been made to contact copyright holders of any material reproduced in this book. Any omissions will be rectified in subsequent printings if notice is given to the publishers.

Some words are shown in bold, **like this.** You can find out what they mean by looking in the Glossary.

Contents

What Is Racism?

"Racist" people believe that personality and behavior are linked to physical characteristics. Because they believe in this link, racists base their judgment of a person's abilities or intelligence on the shape of that person's face or on skin color. Racists are also usually convinced that other **ethnic groups** or **nationalities** are inferior to their own. This false attitude of superiority is another facet of racism.

Racism can take the form of a casual joke between friends, using **stereotypes** as the basis for the joke; it can be reflected in graffiti on a street wall, or chants at a football game. At its most extreme, racism may mean that someone is murdered because of the color of his or her skin.

What is racial discrimination?

Direct racial **discrimination** is a kind of demeaning behavior that treats one person less favorably than another on grounds of race, color, nationality, or ethnic origins.

Indirect racial discrimination happens when people are treated according to the same rules as everyone else, but the effect of the rules is to disadvantage that particular racial group. For example, to refuse a person a job because of his or her skin tone is **direct discrimination.** But if gaining a position at a job is restricted to people who attended a particular school, and that school has always had only white or nearly all white students, this is known as **indirect discrimination.**

What is ethnicity?

An ethnic group shares a cultural or national history, such as **Roma** peoples, Spanish-Americans and citizens of Polish descent in the United States, citizens of Italian descent in Australia, and **Kosovans** in Great Britain.

"All human beings are born free and equal, without distinction of any kind, such as race, color, sex, language, religion, political or other opinion, national or social origin, property, birth, or other status."

From the Universal Declaration of Human Rights, United Nations (1948)

4

What is institutional racism?

When the policies of an institution, such as a business or a public office, encourage racially discriminatory results, even if the people working in that institution are not racists, institutional racism is said to exist.

Racism can extend beyond the actions of individuals and disrupt **communities** in many ways. History shows that some of the worst crimes against humanity have been committed by governments that have created societies based on racism. For much of the 20th century, the **apartheid** regime in South Africa treated black people as inferior to whites. In Nazi Germany between 1933 and 1945, and more recently in the countries that used to make up Yugoslavia, the political leaders and governments persecuted and killed entire communities because they belonged to a certain "race." This ugly extreme of racism is called "ethnic cleansing" or **"genocide."**

This racist graffiti was spray-painted on a wall in Poland.

When racism surfaces, as at this demonstration in Britain, it creates racial tension and often leads to violence.

5

Race and Racists

Racism: a fact of history

Racism is one of the most important issues facing the world today. It affects the schools we go to, sports we follow, **communities** we call home, and countries we live in. Some people are affected or oppressed by racism every single day. **Oppression** stops them from achieving their individual potential and pursuing their dreams, and makes their lives miserable.

By looking at the past we can often find similarities or connections that help our understanding of the world today. The history of racism reminds us that terrible acts of violence and suffering can grow from a fear or dislike of people who are "different." But it is also important to remember that reacting against racism has sparked positive changes in **civil** and **human rights.**

Learning from the past

We only need to look around our own community—friends at school, people on television, or next-door neighbors—to see how incredibly diverse people are. In fact, with more and more people from varying ethnic backgrounds living side by side, our societies are more diverse now than ever. Our lives are enriched and inspired by athletes, writers, artists, and musicians who have succeeded in multiethnic societies. But racism is far from being a thing of the past: **discrimination,** hate crimes, and racial violence are facts of the present day. Since the 1940s the **United Nations** has encouraged **democracies** throughout the world to pass laws making racial discrimination unlawful. Today free, democratic societies such as those of the United States, Europe, and Australia have passed civil rights and racial discrimination acts that make any sort of racist behavior unlawful, whether it happens at work, in school, or on the streets.

This book will look at periods of history that showed the world how ugly racism can be, and will illustrate why it is so important to make sure that racism is unlawful. It will also explain how racism affects our societies today, and why it is still important for us to recognize and tackle this kind of discrimination.

Persecuted because of their "race": prisoners of war stand behind barbed wire fences in the Auschwitz concentration camp during World War II.

❝I hate racial discrimination most intensely and all its manifestations. . . . I have cherished the ideal of a democratic and free society in which all persons live together in harmony and with equal opportunities.❞

Nelson Mandela, president of South Africa from 1994 to 1999. Mandela was elected to office in South Africa's first ever multiracial elections.

What Is Race?

For some people, race starts with the family: who their parents are, or their grandparents or great-great grandparents. The various members of a person's family tree provide that person with valuable information about the makeup of his or her **genes** and **DNA.** The chemicals in a person's DNA carry information from one generation to the next, from parents to children. This inherited information, a sort of personal map or an individual's **genome,** helps explain why children often look like their parents, or why brothers and sisters may have the same color eyes. It also means that a person's physical features such as shape of face and body, color of hair, skin, or eyes, are inherited from his or her ancestors. The inheritance of physical features is known as heredity.

Beyond the family

Today the world's population is more than six billion, but every person on the planet is unique, with his or her very own genome (although identical twins share a genome). Despite this incredible diversity, all humans belong to the same group, or **species,** called *Homo sapiens*. This common name means that *all* of us share biological and genetic similarities. When people think about "race" in this way, they often say things like: "We're all part of the human race," or "We're all human beings."

However, some people understand the word "race" to mean a certain group defined by certain physical characteristics, for example, black people in the United States, or every white person in Sydney, Australia. This way of understanding race can link a person's appearance with their personality or their ability. For example, someone might say: "All Asian kids are good at math," or

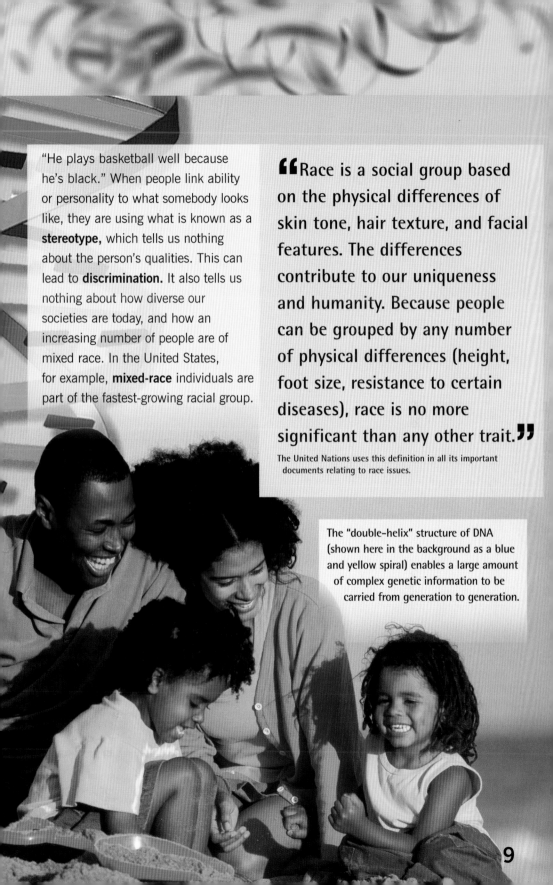

"He plays basketball well because he's black." When people link ability or personality to what somebody looks like, they are using what is known as a **stereotype,** which tells us nothing about the person's qualities. This can lead to **discrimination.** It also tells us nothing about how diverse our societies are today, and how an increasing number of people are of mixed race. In the United States, for example, **mixed-race** individuals are part of the fastest-growing racial group.

❝Race is a social group based on the physical differences of skin tone, hair texture, and facial features. The differences contribute to our uniqueness and humanity. Because people can be grouped by any number of physical differences (height, foot size, resistance to certain diseases), race is no more significant than any other trait.❞

The United Nations uses this definition in all its important documents relating to race issues.

The "double-helix" structure of DNA (shown here in the background as a blue and yellow spiral) enables a large amount of complex genetic information to be carried from generation to generation.

The Slave Trade

Slavery is the situation that arises when one person has absolute power over another. Slavery has existed for centuries. Throughout its long history, people have been forced to work in extremely harsh conditions for little or no pay. Descriptions of slavery can be found in the Bible and the Koran, and it existed in the Greek empire (800–146 B.C.E.) and the Roman empire (753 B.C.E.–C.E. 455). West African kingdoms also kept slaves, and a thriving trade in East Africa was driven by sultans from the Middle East, who sold people from across Persia (present-day Iran) and Mesopotamia (present-day Iraq). But although these examples of slavery led to people being treated terribly, historians do not consider them to be acts of racism. This is because the slave traders and masters were often from the same **ethnic** or racial **group** as the slaves. This was not, however, the case with the Atlantic Slave Trade.

Starting in the 16th century and involving several European countries, the Atlantic Slave Trade was the forced movement of people from Africa to the Americas. Although Arab and African traders were involved in capturing and selling slaves, the main driving force was Europe's demand for plantation workers in the Caribbean, Brazil, and what is now North America. The European nations gained huge economic benefits from the slave trade.

Shackled on the shores of West Africa, men are paraded like goods in front of a slave trader at the height of the Atlantic Slave Trade in 1820.

Money made from slavery helped to finance the **Industrial Revolution** in Britain during the 18th century.

For the African people who were captured and sold into slavery, the experience was inhumane. Each ship crossing the "Middle Passage" (a name given to the Atlantic journey) carried between 250 and 600 people in very cramped conditions. Men were chained together, and women were transported in separate parts of the ships. The average voyage took from 5 to 12 weeks, during which at least 1 million people died from diseases such as **dysentery** and **smallpox.** Those who survived were put to work on cotton, tobacco, sugar, and rice plantations, and were often treated cruelly by the European and American plantation owners. Some historians estimate that, between the years 1450 and 1850, at least 12 million people were shipped across the Atlantic. Other historians think that, in the same period, as many as 28 million people left Africa in 54,000 separate voyages.

"We ought to be considered as men"

Toward the end of the 18th century, "slave uprisings" in the West Indies and a growing **abolitionist** movement in Europe marked the beginning of the end for slavery. The trade was abolished in Britain in 1807.

In 1861 the American Civil War began. According to Abraham Lincoln, who had just become the sixteenth president of the United States, this war was fought because: "Government cannot endure permanently half slave, half free." The bloody conflict took more than 600,000 American lives. When it ended in 1865, slavery was abolished via the Thirteenth Amendment to the Constitution. The Fourteenth (1868) and Fifteenth (1870) Amendments granted African Americans U.S. citizenship and the right to vote.

❝I looked around the ship. . . . With the loathsomeness of the stench and the crying together, I became so sick and low that I was not able to eat. . . . I now wished for the last friend, Death, to relieve me.❞

From *The Interesting Narrative of the Life of Olaudah Equiano* (1789). Books such as this, written by former slaves, helped to bring about an end to slavery. They drew people's attention to its cruel and inhumane practices.

Colonialism

At the end of the 1800s, many peoples in Africa, Asia, Australia, and the West Indies were directly ruled by countries in Europe. They became known as "colonies" or "empires." The powers that ruled these colonies included Britain, France, Spain, Germany, Holland, Belgium, and Italy, with Britain controlling the largest empire. These powers believed that the colonies they governed were in need of European "civilization" and were eager to develop economies, provide medicine, and encourage education there. The colonial governments also wanted to increase their own wealth and power by exploiting the colonies. Many political and business leaders believed that if Europe's economy was to continue to grow, it needed extra resources, such as cotton or steel, many of which could be obtained from the colonized lands.

Much of this colonial activity took place without the agreement of the local inhabitants. For example, when English ships first arrived in Australia in 1788, the Aboriginal people weren't consulted when the English settlers "claimed" the land. African peoples experienced similar treatment. At a conference in Berlin in 1884, the European colonial powers gathered to decide the national borders of the continent. Without the permission or involvement of the African peoples, the European leaders decided which portions of land should be allocated to the various European governments, and Africa was "sliced up like a cake."

German missionaries prepare to take over administration of the East Africa colony in 1891. Missionary camps such as these were scattered throughout the German empire.

Africa: the white man's burden

Throughout the 1700s European leaders had encouraged early explorers in Africa to "open the path for commerce and Christianity." To raise money for these journeys, adventurers and missionaries often publicized their trips as the "white man's burden." By this they meant they believed that Africa was shrouded by ignorance (referring to it as a "dark continent") and that it was Europe's duty to free the "native" people of "heathen" religions. When the famous British explorer, David Livingstone, died in 1862, he requested that his tombstone should bear words to encourage others in Europe to follow his example, and rescue the "natives" from the "sore of the world."

What the European explorers and leaders were blind to, however, were historical facts. Across Africa, Asia, and Australia, advanced cultures already existed with their own distinct societies, art forms, and religious beliefs. Instead of bringing "civilization," the Europeans tended to bring culture-clash and devastation, even war. Battles were fought against the Zulus in southern Africa and Emperor Menelik of Abyssinia (already an ancient Christian kingdom). Instead of the word of the Bible, it was the power of the "Maxim" machine gun that enabled the Europeans to colonize parts of Africa.

Once colonial powers had settled, however, there were benefits. Some local people took European-style jobs as police officers, soldiers, or government clerks. There was an enormous amount of building: railroads in eastern and southern Africa, roads, bridges, and factories. Healthcare and education programs helped to control diseases and encouraged children to read and write. But despite all this, racial **segregation** and **discrimination** loomed large in colonial society. European colonial **communities** lived separately from black communities, with white people enjoying the best conditions.

Native Americans

In 1883 the U.S. government's Indian Religious Crimes Code virtually outlawed the religious beliefs of some 240 different tribal groups across North America, particularly those of the Plains tribes. Under the Code, the U.S. government established Courts of Indian Offenses to enforce "civilized habits and pursuits."

The "Science" of Race

The origin and **evolution** of human beings has fascinated, baffled, and intrigued people for centuries. In the 17th century, scientists such as Swedish-born Carolus Linnaeus (1707–1778) and French-born George Cuvier (1769–1832) designed elaborate ways of classifying the natural world, beginning with descriptions of the physical features of plants and animals. By the 19th century, *Homo sapiens* was also classified and divided into race categories like "negroid," "mongoloid," and "caucasoid." The science of race was born, and so were beliefs that help to explain the idea of European superiority during the Atlantic Slave Trade and colonialism.

This botanical chart is an example from Carolus Linnaeus's *Systema Naturae*.

When Charles Darwin published *On the Origin of Species* in 1859, he declared that: "Light will be thrown on the origin of man and his history." But Darwin's description of evolution as the "survival of the fittest" led some people to believe that the various human race categories were in an evolutionary battle. This misreading of Darwin's writing encouraged and supported several European "scientists" who believed that some human beings and races were more evolved than others. This way of thinking, which became known as **Social Darwinism,** tended to place white Europeans higher up the human evolutionary tree. Some even believed you could tell how "evolved" or "civilized" people were by measuring the size of their skulls.

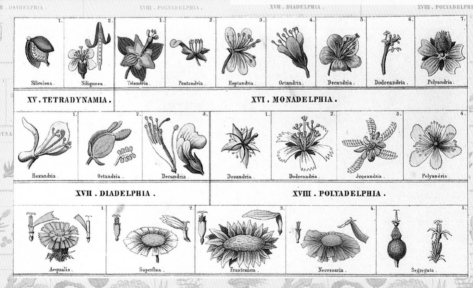

Race: the "pseudo science"

After World War II, a group of leading British scientists argued, by using modern **genetics,** that there wasn't any real science behind race theories. Because human beings had **migrated** across the Earth for thousands of years, it was impossible to classify people into "races." They suggested the term "**ethnic group**" be used instead of the word "race." Unlike "race," which uses biological or physical characteristics to describe individual or group identity, the term "ethnic group" emphasizes the national and cultural factors. The **United Nations** supported this categorization, adding that there was "no scientific evidence to prove humans differ in intelligence or emotional development based on race." The ideas that may have seemed useful to people in the 1700s and 1800s are now considered "**pseudo** science" or "scientific racism."

Darwin's thinking

In his writings Charles Darwin said that "natural selection" was the driving power behind plant and animal evolution. He said that all organisms were in a constant struggle with others in the same species, and that those that survived through successive generations did so because of biological or physical traits that aided their survival. His ideas led some people to believe that the various human race categories were also in a battle for survival. They were adopted by several European "scientists" who believed that some human beings and races were more evolved than others. But these theories about human evolution were a misinterpretation of Darwin's theory. Darwin's view of nature was not of a superior society, more perfect personality, or more civilized culture, but an entire **species** constantly adapting to changing environments in an endless process of evolution.

The observations and drawings that European explorers made during their travels influenced the science of race. Images of "exotic" or "barbaric" people from other parts of the world fueled the sense of European superiority.

Government of Race: Nazi Germany

After World War I, an atmosphere of social and economic depression existed in Europe. In this unstable climate, **fascist** (extremist) political ideas flourished. **Anti-Semitic** thinking became widespread across Europe and America. Anti-Semitism also surfaced in South Africa, underlying the ideas of racial **segregation** that separated black and white **communities.** In Germany, the writings and rousing speeches of a young politician named Adolph Hitler began to attract attention.

In a book called *Mein Kampf* (My Struggle), Hitler blamed Germany's economic problems on "criminals, Jews, Gypsies, **mixed-race** Negroes, and the feeble-minded." Using ideas of **Social Darwinism,** Hitler falsely claimed that the **Aryan** (racially "pure") culture of Germany was "stronger" and must "dominate." He said that the non-Aryan races, particularly Jewish people, were trying to weaken and destroy the "Volk" (Germanic race).

Racist laws

When the Nazi Party came to power in Germany in 1933, Hitler's "vision" was spread through **propaganda**—speeches on the radio, articles in newspapers, and even in children's nursery rhymes. But it was laws made by the Nazis that confirmed Germany's government of race. These included the Nuremberg Laws on Citizenship and Race (1935), which banned interracial marriage, forced non-Aryans to use separate seats on buses and park benches, and ruled that non-Aryans could not vote. The Nuremberg laws also deprived German Jews of their right to German citizenship.

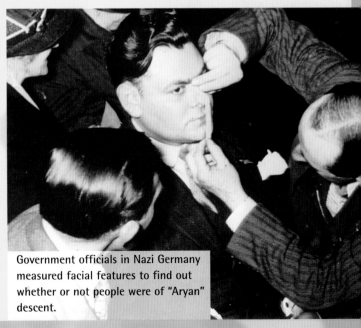

Government officials in Nazi Germany measured facial features to find out whether or not people were of "Aryan" descent.

Kristallnacht

One night in November 1938, mobs of angry protesters took to the streets to avenge the death of a German diplomat, alleged to have been murdered by a young Jewish man in Paris. In all, 91 people were killed, while synagogues, shops, and homes were destroyed. So much shattered glass covered the streets the following morning that the night became known as Kristallnacht ("Night of Broken Glass").

In the months that followed Kristallnacht, all Jews were forced to wear a yellow "Star of David" sewn to their clothes. In the face of such harassment and **discrimination,** many fled to seek refuge in Britain, the United States, and France. Many of those who remained were forced into **ghettos** and **concentration camps.** At the Wannsee Conference in 1942, the Nazis made plans to exterminate all Jewish people in Europe. This "Final Solution" led to Jews being sent to execution camps in Poland and Germany. Only after the end of World War II did people find out that more than six million Jewish children, men, and women had been killed.

Not only did the Nazis divide society, they also systematically organized the mass killing of Jewish people. Forced to wear the Star of David, these families arrive at Auschwitz death camp in 1944.

"Separate Development" in South Africa

As the world recovered from the shock of **genocide** in Europe, the Afrikaner Nationalist Party (ANP) gained support for ideas of **apartheid** (or "apartness") in South Africa. The ANP won the 1948 election in South Africa with slogans suggesting that "white civilization" must not disappear under a "black sea." In 1950 the Population Registration Act put all the people into racial categories. Interracial marriage was made illegal, and nonwhites were not allowed to vote or join political parties. Soon the whole of South African society was involved in "separate development," with separate housing, transportation, drinking fountains, schools, and healthcare for whites and nonwhites. Though the black population made up more than 75 percent of South Africa's total population, black people were only allowed to use 13 percent of the land. The white population, which made up less than 15 percent of the total population, was allocated 87 percent of the land.

Resisting Racism

While apartheid divided South African society, a growing **civil rights** movement responded to racism in the United States. How, asked African-American activists, could the United States promote a system of racial injustice, especially after having helped to defeat Hitler? How could the United States still enforce "**Jim Crow**" **laws** enacted by some southern states expressly to enforce **segregation** that effectively kept black children from attending the better, all-white state schools since the end of the Civil War?

"We shall overcome"

These questions were not new. Since the beginning of the 20th century, political and **civil rights** groups had been working to combat racism in the United States. Since 1909 the National Association for the Advancement of Colored People (NAACP) had held regular meetings and published their own magazine. But after World War II, a wave of civil rights activity spread across the country.

In 1947 the Congress of Racial Equality (CORE) organized the first "Journeys of Reconciliation" (popularly known as "Freedom Rides"). The idea was to challenge the segregation on public transportation, particularly in southern states. CORE sent eight white men and eight black men to travel on public buses across Kentucky, Tennessee, North Carolina, and Virginia. A number of the black activists were arrested several times for using the whites-only transportation. These journeys made the headlines in newspapers, on television, and on radio. The publicity encouraged other groups, such as the Southern Christian Leadership Conference (SCLC, founded in 1957) and the Student Nonviolent Coordinating Committee (SNCC, founded in 1960) to organize demonstrations and **boycotts** that challenged racial inequality. These included "sit-in" protests at restaurants for whites only, more freedom rides on buses and trains, and "freedom schools" that taught black history and challenged **discrimination** in American society.

Some of the greatest achievements were made in the law courts. For example, in the 1954 Brown versus Board of Education case, the Supreme Court decided that racial segregation in schools was against the Fourteenth Amendment (promising protection by the government if a citizen's rights are threatened). This was a great boost for civil rights, and encouraged a school in Little Rock, Arkansas, in 1957 to become the first nonsegregated high school.

A beacon for the world

In 1963, 200,000 people marched in a peaceful demonstration to Washington, D.C. They were protesting against segregation laws that still existed in parts of the United States. It was here that civil rights leader Martin Luther King Jr. gave his inspirational "I Have a Dream" speech. In 1964 Congress passed the Civil Rights Act, which made discrimination in public places illegal. This was an inspiration for many **communities** in the country, including Hispanics, Native Americans, and those who challenged other kinds of discrimination such as **sexism** and **homophobia.** By now the rest of the world was listening. In the 1960s Australian activists staged freedom rides similar to those in the United States to help Aboriginal people overcome racism there.

The Freedom Rides didn't go unchallenged by racist groups. After being surrounded by a mob of white people near Anniston, Alabama, in May 1961, this bus was firebombed.

> **"I have a dream that my four children will one day live in a nation where they will not be judged by the color of their skin but by the content of their character."**
>
> Martin Luther King Jr. (1963)

Martin Luther King Jr. leads a U.S. civil rights march in the 1960s.

Our Multiethnic

People have been **migrating** all over the world for centuries.
They may be fleeing natural disaster, racial **segregation** or
war, or seeking out economic opportunity and an improved
standard of life. Whether they migrated originally because of
the Atlantic Slave Trade, or as Jewish people fleeing
persecution, or as colonists in Australia and Africa, this
movement of people explains why places like New York in the
United States or London in Britain are so diverse.

A diverse society is made up of people with varying ethnic
backgrounds. This diversity is often described as
"multiethnic," "multiracial," or "multicultural." We can use
these terms to describe the neighborhood, town, city, or
country we live in. Society benefits from this ethnic diversity
in many ways: in music, in business, on the sports field, and
in politics. It makes all our lives richer and more interesting,
extending our range of tastes, ideas, arts, and beliefs.

When people describe themselves as African American,
Chinese, French Canadian, or Mexican American, they're often
explaining who they are and where they come from. And it's
just as important for a country to have an identity. Take, for
example, the United States's identity as a land of opportunity.
Countless immigrants and refugees have arrived here, under
the inscription on the Statue of Liberty that says: "Give me
your tired, your poor, your huddled masses yearning to breathe
free." How we view our country helps us form ideas of what
kind of society we believe we live in, and whether it's fair and
equal.

Ethnic diversity

• Ethnic minorities, including people of non-European descent, make up about 30 percent of the U.S. population—more than 84 million people. African Americans make up 12.1 percent, Hispanic people 12.5 percent, Asians and Pacific islanders 3.7 percent, Native Americans 0.7 percent, and 1.8 percent of another race or identified with more than one race.

• The diversity index was created in the United States to measure how racially and ethnically diverse the population is. In 2000 the diversity index was 49. That means that the chances of two randomly chosen U.S. residents being from different ethnic backgrounds is 49 out of 100, or almost 1 in 2.

• The number of U.S. residents who speak a language other than English at home increased by 47 percent during the 1990s. Over the past 20 years, the number of minority language speakers who are fluent in English has increased at about the same rate as that of those who speak languages other than English at home.

Tension in the melting pot

Across the world many societies are now multiethnic. Some are more successful than others in achieving internal peace and equality, but everywhere there are problems encouraged by small groups of extremists. Most recently, in the United States following the destruction of the World Trade Center on September 11, 2001, hate crimes against Arab Americans increased dramatically in spite of calls for calm from leaders. These crimes included unprovoked slayings in many places, as well as acts of vandalism against Arab Americans or those perceived to look like Arabs. In Salt Lake City, the restaurant business of a Pakistani family that had lived in the states for fifteen years was set on fire by a man who "knew that the owners were from the same area of the world the bombing suspects came from." In Seattle a man was charged with shooting at worshipers at a mosque and attempting to torch the building.

Federal crime statistics show that hate crimes have traditionally been targeted against African Americans, Hispanics, Jews, Asian Americans, and Native Americans. Until recently few such attacks have been targeted against people of Arab descent or of the Muslim faith. In turbulent times such as the months following the World Trade Center disaster, reason can give way to **xenophobia,** or fear of the unknown.

What about today?

Today there is still widespread discrimination in many areas, and racial violence and harassment continue to be a problem. "Hate crimes," such as physical attacks, verbal abuse, or racially motivated murders, happen all over the world, though sometimes they go unreported. The African-American statesman Colin Powell may be one of the most powerful leaders in the White House, but ordinary citizens like Rodney King (see page 25) are still attacked and even murdered because of the color of their skin.

Across Europe political parties like the Front Nationale (FN) of France, the Austrian Freedom Party (FPO), or Danish Peoples' Party (DPP) blame immigration for social problems, sometimes adding that all African, Asian, and Arab Muslim people should be "sent home." The Internet is used to send racist messages across the world, while in Europe racist groups use firebombs and nailbombs to attack ethnic minorities. In Australia some Aboriginal **communities** don't believe they are being treated fairly because they don't have equal access to education, housing, or healthcare. And after the attack on September 11, 2001, on the World Trade Center, Muslims in Europe as well as the United States have experienced increased hostility.

There were 25,000 mourners at the funeral of a Turkish woman who was killed, along with four others, in a racist firebomb attack in the German town of Solingen. The peaceful funeral later became violent when some members of the crowd, unable to contain their anger and outrage, overturned cars, looted stores, and smashed windows.

Crimes of hate

• In the year 2000, 9,430 hate crimes were reported to law enforcement agencies in the United States.

• 65 percent of these crimes were directed at individuals; 34.4 percent were against property.

• 32.1 percent occurred in or around residential properties, while 17.4 percent occurred on the street or on highways.

Racism and the Legal System

Most people experience the legal system in a variety of ways. It could be anything from an encounter with a neighborhood police officer or judge in a courthouse, to the way in which prisons are run or governments handle drug problems. If racism affects any part of this legal system, peoples' **civil rights** are threatened and entire **communities** may lose faith in justice and feel excluded from society.

Racial profiling

Although it is illegal, many police departments have been known to use racial profiling to catch criminals. This means that the police will stop and search any person they suspect might be guilty. In the United States,

government studies show that black people are several times more likely to be stopped and searched than white people. This evidence of "racial profiling" supports the claims of those communities who accuse the police of **discrimination.** And because it happens on the street, face-to-face, it can generate a lot of anger among ethnic minorities.

In police custody

When a person is stopped or arrested by a member of the police force, it means that they are in "police custody." Occasionally people are injured, or even killed, while in police custody. The **human rights** group Amnesty International has claimed that, in

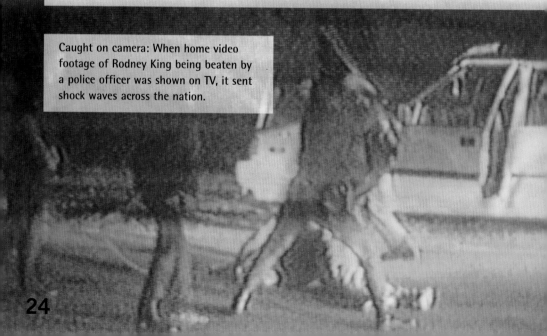

Caught on camera: When home video footage of Rodney King being beaten by a police officer was shown on TV, it sent shock waves across the nation.

Austria, police aren't likely to be taken to court if they assault members of ethnic minorities while they are in custody. If a white person is assaulted, however, an officer is more likely to go to court. This inequality can create racial tension in society. For example, in Los Angeles in 1991, four police officers were accused of assaulting Rodney King, a black citizen, while he was in police custody. An amateur video of the attack was used as evidence against the police officers when the case was brought to court. Despite this evidence, which had also been broadcast throughout the country on news programs, the jury decided to **acquit** three of the officers. This decision sparked violent rioting in Los Angeles that resulted in 2,000 injuries, four deaths, and $990 million worth of damage.

When the system fails

Communities have often criticized the police for not taking racist crimes seriously enough. In Britain in 1992, a teenager named Stephen Lawrence died as the result of an unprovoked racist attack. The police were slow to find the killers, so the family decided to start their own investigation. The Lawrences didn't manage to convict the suspects, but their efforts drew attention to the police handling of the case. The British government began to ask why the police had acted so unprofessionally, and in 1999 accused the British police force of institutional racism.

> **❝This society has stood by and allowed my son's killers to make a mockery of the law.❞**
>
> Doreen Lawrence, mother of Stephen Lawrence, speaking about the British government inquiry in 1999

Stephen Lawrence's parents, Doreen and Neville, refused to accept the way in which the police had dealt with their son's death.

Racism at Work

Civil rights laws have made racial **discrimination** at work unlawful. Most companies also know that it is better for business to employ people that reflect the society as a whole. In a diverse society, companies do better if equal opportunities are given to people of all ethnic backgrounds. But despite this, the facts show that racial discrimination still exists at work.

For example, in the United States an annual report published in 2002 and entitled "The State of Black America" revealed that 10.2 percent of African Americans were unemployed, while 5.2 percent—about half the number—of the white population was out of work. In home ownership, another indicator of economic progress, 74 percent of whites owned their own homes compared to only 48 percent of blacks. In Britain in the mid-1990s, there were more than 1,300 registered cases of people who alleged they'd been racially discriminated against. Although racism at work can sometimes be difficult to notice or to prove, most of these cases are examples of **direct discrimination**.

Direct discrimination

An organization monitoring equal opportunities opened a telephone hotline in Britain to find out about racism at work. In just five days they had received 450 calls. A black civil servant described how he'd been turned down for promotion, despite having the right qualifications. He discovered that a white person without qualifications had been given the job. When he complained, he eventually got the job, but his boss said how much he "hated the black race coming in here to take jobs." This upset the civil servant a great deal, especially since he'd been living in the country for nearly 40 years. Another call was from a machine operator, who said people at the factory he worked at called him racist names. He had been forced to start working the night shift to avoid harassment.

These examples of direct racism are very stressful to those people who experience them. Some people become so depressed that they have to leave their jobs or take days off to recover. This is bad for the atmosphere of any workplace, and bad for business, too.

❝Our past, your future.❞

NAACP slogan

The NAACP (National Association for the Advancement of Colored People) has been involved in positive change for African Americans and cooperation between ethnic groups since its inception in 1909.

Racism and Sports

Sports can bring people together. They offer an opportunity for ability to speak louder than racial **prejudice.** Sports are also part of a country's "cultural fabric," something that people like to talk about and share experiences of at school and work, on buses, trains, and street corners. To some fans, sports are almost like a religion. Of course, sports are also about winning, but the greatest sports personalities, from Muhammad Ali to Tiger Woods, often talk about the atmosphere and the spirit of the sport. And it's this spirit that can be spoiled by racism.

Tiger Woods, widely regarded as the best golfer of all time, is presented with the ceremonial green jacket after winning the U.S. Masters tournament for the third time in 2002.

However, sometimes athletes themselves can display racist behavior. Prior to the Sydney Olympics in 2000, an Australian athlete said, "You can pretty much knock out all the dark guys." He was referring to the fact that the conditions in Australia were better for him (a white athlete) than for African Americans. The Australian Olympic Committee apologized for the remark, but an American athlete said it would "create animosity between the United States and Australia." And there was the instance of an American Major League baseball player, John Rocker, who was not even talking about baseball, but who offended people by saying: "The biggest thing I don't like about New York are the foreigners. I'm not a very big fan of foreigners."

After a great deal of controversy, Rocker was fined and made to apologize publicly. His performance subsequently declined and he was demoted to the minor leagues at great loss to his career.

A very small minority of sports fans throughout the world see sporting events as an opportunity to stir up racial hatred, especially at soccer matches between rival countries.

"You are a disgrace to the game of baseball. Maybe you should think before you shoot off your big fat mouth. Get some class!"
A New York Mets fan to John Rocker

The Media and Race

In a "multimedia age," the images on television and movie screens and the information we read in newspapers or on the Internet shape our opinions and our societies. Racism can be a part of the media in different ways. There are examples of **direct racism** on the Internet, shown through the growth of "hate sites." Certain kinds of language used by news reporters can stir up an atmosphere of racial tension in society (see pages 32–33). And it is commonly the case that television and radio programs don't reflect the diversity of society. Although people like Oprah Winfrey, Bill Cosby, or Will Smith are very successful, the U.S. media still tends to be dominated by white people. One reason for this is that the companies that pay to advertise their products in the media still tend to direct their advertising at affluent whites. And although people from ethnic minorities may watch television

shows with predominantly white casts, such as *Buffy the Vampire Slayer* or *Friends*, white audiences tend not to watch shows with mainly African American or Hispanic casts.

Racial stereotypes

The people and characters we see on television or in the movies are often role models for us. But members of the Hispanic **community,** for example, complain that they are **stereotyped** by being given small or negative roles like criminals or drug dealers. Similar criticism has been directed at Australian television for stereotyping Aboriginal communities. Even after the end of **apartheid** in South Africa, an independent government organization, the Human Rights Commission, recently criticized the media for regularly using racial stereotypes and not taking news stories about some communities seriously enough.

Many people feel that popular TV shows should reflect diversity in society, but this doesn't always happen.

Trouble at the top?

Who decides what sort of programs should be on television, or what kind of characters will be in the movies? These decisions are made by "people at the top"—producers, screenwriters, news reporters, and directors. The results don't mean that these people are racist, but simply that they don't reflect the diversity of society.

For example, in 2001 Greg Dyke of the BBC (British Broadcasting Company) said that the organization was "hideously white." There are far more white people than black or Asian people working at the BBC, and this means that characters on television can become stereotyped, and the programs may be out of step with the diverse nature of society. Dyke's criticism suggested that most high-ranking executives and producers are too often white (and male).

Oprah Winfrey has become one of the most powerful and wealthy media figures in the United States.

❝ . . . [E]very form of media is failing to deliver an accurate picture of our diverse society, and because of this, some of our citizens are slow to understand and accept other cultures.❞

Sir Herman Ouseley, Chairman of the British Commission for Racial Equality

The Media and Migration

There are many reasons why people move away from their homes. Some have fled war or racial persecution in their own countries, others are escaping poverty or want to improve life for themselves and their families. The reasons differ from person to person, but the arrival of **migrants** into countries is a hotly debated issue. Politicians might ask: "Will immigrants put a strain on society? Or do they improve an economy and enrich culture?" The media also fuels the debate, with images of people crossing the border from Mexico into the United States, or reports about refugees arriving in boats off the Australian coast. The "heat" of these debates can create tension in society, and sometimes media coverage only makes things worse.

A hostile reception

In 1998 **Roma** and **Kosovan** migrants began to arrive in Britain from Eastern Europe, fleeing persecution in their own countries and seeking **asylum.** In reaction, a local newspaper in the south of England began publishing articles that said things like: "We are left with the backdraft of human sewage and no cash to wash it down the drain." The articles called the migrants "bootleggers, scum-of-the-earth drug smugglers," and the newspaper defended its stance, saying it was "their right to freedom of speech," and that they were "reflecting the opinion of the area." Soon, national newspapers began to print similar articles. Ironically, this sort of **xenophobia** echoed the rantings of Adolph Hitler, whom Britain had sacrificed so much to defeat only decades before.

Border officials try to control the flow of people crossing between Mexico and the Southwest.

Can words create violence?

At the same time, there was an increase in the number of attacks on migrant families. Some had fireworks put through their mailboxes, bottles smashed against their windows, or threatening slogans painted on their doors. This sort of violence began to spread in Britain. Often the victims weren't even migrants, but had been attacked because of how they looked. In August 2000 an asylum seeker was murdered and two others were stabbed within three days of one another.

In April 2001 a **European Union** report was published that criticized the British media for the way in which they reported the arrival of migrants. It said that an atmosphere of racial tension had been created by "intolerant coverage of these groups of persons in the media." In 2002 Kris Janowski, the **United Nations** High Commissioner for Refugees, told the French news agency, Agence France Presse: "We do think there is a linkage between the notoriously negative portrayal of asylum-seekers in the media and this kind of violence."

Young Muslims gather in Australia in August 2001. They are asking the Australian government to allow a ferry carrying 460 asylum seekers from Afghanistan to land on Christmas Island.

Citizens of the World?

As societies around the world continue to become increasingly multi-ethnic, the arguments about racism become less about whether it is wrong or right. Instead the most pressing problem is how to ensure that diverse **communities** live without racial tension, in a society free of racial **prejudice** and **discrimination.** This chapter looks at the different opinions and arguments that have surfaced in the search for a multiethnic society in which *everybody* has equal opportunities in life.

A Red Cross "holding station" accommodates refugees in Sangatte, northern France.

Today there are 150 million people living outside their countries of birth. At least 22 million have been forced to move from their homes because of war or racial persecution. We already know that multiethnic societies are built on a history of migration. We also know that the arrival of **migrants** into a society can create racial tension. Some people argue that this tension is the result of a new kind of racism: that of discrimination and prejudice against people who want and need to improve their lives. But whether migration actually does create tension depends on the actions of governments across the world.

Managing migration

Since most of the migrant populations are from less developed countries, some people argue that they bring unskilled and uneducated individuals into society. If migrants have less "economic value," there might be more strain on public services like health, housing, and education. In the United States, for example, economists argue that if the government supports healthcare for Hispanic migrants, then others in society will have to pay more for health insurance. There is also a concern that migrants will become "second-class" citizens, and that **ghetto**-like communities will grow. This division could mean that certain communities are excluded and less likely to become involved in the rest of society. To avoid this, some people think that governments should manage migration by limiting the number of people allowed into a country. They think that governments should only select those individuals who fit the needs of a society, for example, those with skills, such as doctors or computer experts, who can immediately contribute to the economy.

However, some people argue that managed migration makes matters worse. If only skilled migrants are encouraged, then there will be fewer people in less-developed countries where the skills are needed most. This could lead to more poverty and even more people wanting to leave. The **United Nations** also estimates that, by the year 2025, 159 million migrant workers will be needed to keep the European economy growing. This is because birth rates in Europe are falling and there is a need for both skilled and unskilled workers. To keep the European economy growing and to offer improved lifestyles for those in less-developed countries, some argue that it is more sensible to relax migration controls and allow people to move more freely as citizens of the world.

Institutional Racism

The term "institutional racism" was first used by the American activist Stokely Carmichael during the **civil rights** movement in the 1950s and 1960s. Institutional racism refers to racism that exists anywhere in an organization, from the daily running of a small business to the way in which people are treated in a large concern such as the criminal justice system. Institutional racism may be evident in the lunchroom at work, where racist jokes or **stereotypes** are accepted by employees. It might also mean that the opportunities people have while working for an organization are unequal. Or it may mean that a police force is prejudiced in the way in which it investigates crime within a certain **community.**

Too much pressure?

Some politicians and journalists argue that if a police force is accused of institutional racism, then it's even less likely that ethnic minorities will want to work for it. They also say that instructing the police force to "clean up its act" can put too much pressure on officers. For example, after the Stephen Lawrence case in Britain, a police chief admitted: "We failed. We could and should have done better." But according to critics, the media attention and public pressure that followed the Lawrence inquiry actually led to an increase in the number of street crimes affecting all citizens. Another leading police official said: "Officers' jobs have been made far more difficult. . . . Police are there to deal with crime; they are not interested in race."

A Moroccan worker is detained by Spanish police following an increase in racial tension and unrest in the town of El Ejido in February 2000.

The British police force has attempted to recruit a variety of ethnic groups as a way of representing the diversity of society and improving relations with citizens.

In the United States, there are similar arguments on the issue of racial profiling. Those people in favor of profiling ask: If more crime is being committed by a certain **ethnic group,** then why is it wrong for a police force to use its limited amount of money and time to stop and search people of a particular ethnic group? If, for example, most drug dealers in an area are known to be black or Hispanic, then more ethnic minorities will show up in the crime figures. These arguments often say that racial profiling is justified, especially if the "greater good" of society is at stake. But critics of racial profiling say it is an example of institutional racism because it is an everyday police practice that also targets innocent people because of the color of their skin.

Although there is disagreement about the ways in which institutional racism should be handled, many people still believe that its "discovery" is a positive step toward tackling **discrimination.** This is mainly because it has brought attention to racist crime in society and challenged discrimination inside large organizations such as the police force and the criminal justice system.

❝The collective failure of an organization to provide an appropriate and professional service to people because of their color, culture, or ethnic origin. It can be seen or detected in the processes, attitudes, and behavior that amount to discrimination through unwitting prejudice, ignorance, thoughtlessness, and racist stereotyping that disadvantage minority ethnic people.❞

Following the death of Stephen Lawrence, a government investigation resulted in a report (quoted above) that accused the British police force of institutional racism.

37

Too black and white?

Some people still think our understanding of racism is too simplistic, often because there is evidence of racism *between* ethnic minorities. For example, there are cases of racial tension between African migrants and British-Caribbean communities in London, or instances of African-American schoolchildren calling Chinese-American students names. These examples show that racism is not just a "black and white" issue, and that it's also important to look for other causes of racial tension that are rooted deep in society.

Society in the spotlight

Some people argue that not everyone in society is given an equal chance to go to a good school, find a good job, or live in a comfortable home. This doesn't just mean inequality for ethnic minorities, it means inequality for poorer white **communities,** too. If people can't find work or send their children to a good school, then a whole community might become depressed. This atmosphere of social depression can lead to more crime and unemployment. When something like this happens to a community, it is less likely that different **ethnic groups** will **integrate** because they blame each other for their problems.

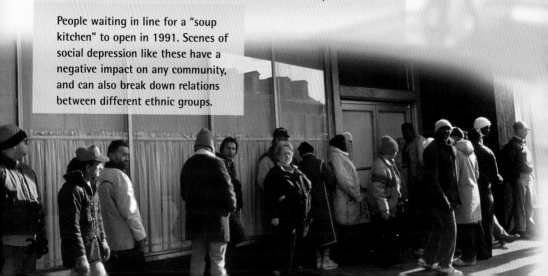

People waiting in line for a "soup kitchen" to open in 1991. Scenes of social depression like these have a negative impact on any community, and can also break down relations between different ethnic groups.

Positive action—a black female police officer distributes antidrug literature to children.

When society is **segregated** like this, relations between the different communities can break down even more quickly and easily, since they have less chance of learning to understand and accept each other. These sorts of problems are often deeply rooted in society, and can take a long time to change. Some people, however, believe that very practical and immediate things can be done. If a community is ethnically diverse, then there should be politicians, police, teachers, doctors, and lawyers who reflect this diversity. If, for example, there were more Hispanic police officers in certain areas of the United States, then a lot of problems and tensions could be resolved before they became another ugly crime figure. This could help restore trust, forging stronger relations between all ethnic groups and helping to build a society where all people are treated fairly, with equal chances to achieve and feel proud about their lives.

❝ . . . [R]acism resides not so much in institutions, but in the hearts and minds of individuals.❞

Journalist Ziauddin Sardar talking about schools in London, 1999

39

The Global Community Against Racism

Since the end of World War II, the **United Nations** has been actively involved in the promotion of **human rights.** In 1948 the UN produced a Universal Declaration of Human Rights (part of it is quoted on page 4) that set new standards. It was followed by a series of more detailed agreements, such as the International Convention on the Elimination of All Forms of Racial Discrimination (1966). The UN has a committee that receives reports from governments and voluntary bodies on the progress being made under this Convention in different states. But the UN does not have any powers of enforcement.

There are also hundreds of nongovernmental organizations (NGOs), such as Amnesty International and Human Rights Watch, that are dedicated to tackling racism. These organizations are independent of governments and carry out their own research into racism. Although they don't have the power to make laws, NGOs have a big influence in providing information to governments and the population as a whole. They work closely with the media, providing information and encouraging newspaper articles and television programs that discuss racism. NGOs also offer support and legal advice to **communities** and individuals affected by racism. The presence of NGOs in society helps make people around the world more aware, and pressures governments to tackle racism.

❝ . . . [I]t can shape and embody the spirit of the new century, based on the shared conviction that we are all members of one human family.❞

United Nations High Commissioner for Human Rights, Secretary-General Mary Robinson, speaking at the World Conference Against Racism in South Africa in 2001

Two thousand people weave their way through the streets of East London to protest against a rise in racist attacks in the area in March 1994.

40

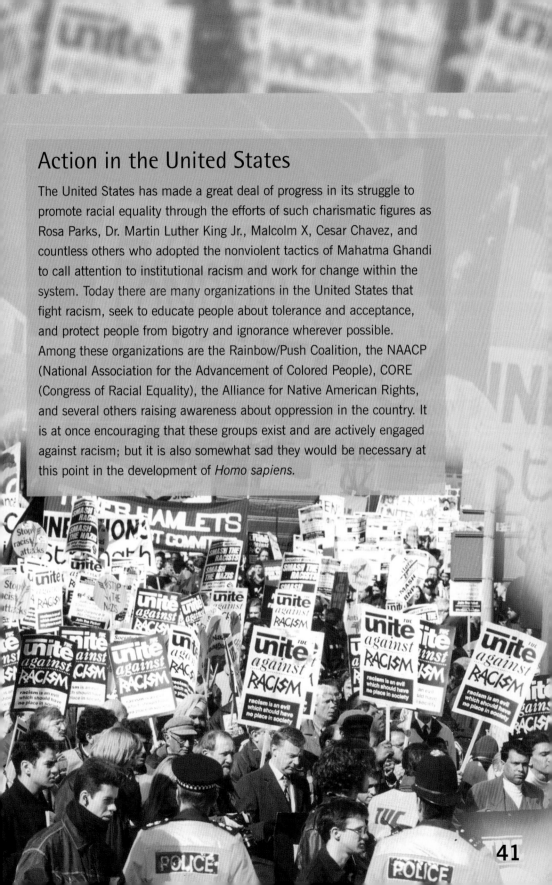

Action in the United States

The United States has made a great deal of progress in its struggle to promote racial equality through the efforts of such charismatic figures as Rosa Parks, Dr. Martin Luther King Jr., Malcolm X, Cesar Chavez, and countless others who adopted the nonviolent tactics of Mahatma Ghandi to call attention to institutional racism and work for change within the system. Today there are many organizations in the United States that fight racism, seek to educate people about tolerance and acceptance, and protect people from bigotry and ignorance wherever possible. Among these organizations are the Rainbow/Push Coalition, the NAACP (National Association for the Advancement of Colored People), CORE (Congress of Racial Equality), the Alliance for Native American Rights, and several others raising awareness about oppression in the country. It is at once encouraging that these groups exist and are actively engaged against racism; but it is also somewhat sad they would be necessary at this point in the development of *Homo sapiens*.

41

The End of Apartheid

The history of South Africa over the past hundred years is an example of how a government based on racist beliefs can be defeated. From the moment that **apartheid** laws were introduced to **segregate** South African society in 1948, they were criticized by people from all walks of life in South Africa and across the world. In 1952 the **United Nations** formally condemned apartheid in South Africa. Throughout the 1950s and 1960s, a growing number of protest marches were held in South Africa. Most were organized by the African National Congress (ANC), a group formed by black South Africans in 1912. The apartheid government opposed these demonstrations by banning the ANC and putting leaders like Nelson Mandela in prison. But the struggle continued.

Sanctions

By the 1980s the world's media was watching South Africa closely, and governments in Europe and the United States were beginning to put economic pressure (sanctions) on the country. Supported by the United Nations, these economic sanctions meant that most countries around the world stopped trading with South Africa. The racial violence worsened, and pressure from the international community increased. Eventually in 1991 the South African president, F.W. de Klerk, lifted the ban on the ANC. At the same time, he began abolishing segregation laws and freed Nelson Mandela from prison (where he'd been for more than 25 years). Although the atmosphere in South Africa was still very tense, Mandela was now free to share his vision of a multiracial, multiethnic future with the South African people and with the rest of the world. He called the new South Africa "Rainbow Nation." In 1994 Mandela was elected president in the first multiracial, democratic elections in South Africa. Although he left office in 1999, he continues to be one of the most inspiring leaders in the world today.

Truth and reconciliation

In 1996 the multiethnic South African government created a new constitution that officially ended apartheid. Since then, one of the most important things that the government has done to help challenge racism is to set up the Truth and Reconciliation Commission (TRC). The TRC was founded in 1995 to help heal South African people of the apartheid years. It became an opportunity for people to find out what **human rights** abuses took place between 1948 and 1994. More importantly it supports apartheid victims with financial aid and helps "restore their dignity." More recently the TRC has supported museums that show the history of apartheid. The hope is that South Africa's troubled past will not be forgotten by future generations.

Nelson Mandela was elected first black president of South Africa in 1994.

❝We have seen a miracle unfold before our very eyes. . . . Freedom and justice must become realities for all our people and we have the privilege of helping to heal the hurts of the past.❞

From the opening speech of the TRC, made by Archbishop Desmond Tutu in 1995

Mrs. Nohle Mohapi becomes the first witness to be sworn in at the Truth and Reconciliation Commission in South Africa in April 1996.

43

Who Else Is Tackling Racism?

Governments and members of the **United Nations** are not the only agencies helping to tackle racism. Politicians themselves recognize that the most effective opposition to racism is achieved by individuals or groups working within a **community.** Today there are literally millions of people around the world helping to challenge racism in their neighborhood, on the Internet, in their schools, in their favorite sports, and in the media.

In communities and schools

People don't just teach antiracism in the classroom; there are examples throughout the world of how schools and youth clubs are tackling racism outside of school. A good example is of students from different schools organizing sporting events or music concerts to raise money for charity and to promote antiracism. This very thing happened in Scotland, after an area had experienced racial tension. An organization called "Kick It Out" helped some local children to stage an antiracism soccer tournament. In the United States, the work of "Artists Against Racism" has encouraged numerous talented musicians and actors to promote antiracism messages and mount antiracism concerts. In some U.S. schools, an organization called ERASE challenges racism by organizing training and activities to promote equality in education.

On the Internet

There are plenty of websites dedicated to tackling racism. Some of these sites provide the latest news on racism issues and encourage antiracist campaigns. There are also sites that encourage people to report racism to their local government.

These are good places to find more information and advice on racism issues, with links to issues across the country. There are also schools and universities, from Pennsylvania in the United States and Newcastle upon Tyne in Britain, to Bangkok in Thailand and Melbourne in Australia, who provide information about racism and guides that help people deal with racism if they experience it firsthand.

What about our governments?

United States

•In 1991 President Bush re-signed the Civil Rights Act. This symbolic gesture was meant to revitalize the civil rights laws passed in the 1960s.

•In 2000 a report was given at the UN as a commitment to eliminate racial **discrimination** in all aspects of U.S. society.

Britain

•In 2000 the Race Relations Act 2000 became law. It declared that all organizations have a positive duty to monitor and promote equality, and it also forbids public authorities to discriminate.

European Union

•During 2000 three important new measures to combat discrimination were adopted by the EU Council of Ministers. For the first time, there will be a comprehensive set of anti-discrimination measures and a minimum standard of legal protection against discrimination.

The Music of Black Origin (MOBO) awards have become a major event in the British music scene.

Ask Yourself: Who Am I?

By learning about the past and becoming more aware of racism issues today, everyone can become part of the **community** of people all over the globe who are challenging racism and intolerance. There are also many other practical things that can be done to confront racism.

Racism reveals itself in facts and figures, but racist behavior always begins with peoples' attitudes. And our attitude toward others is always rooted in who we are. One way to start thinking about who we are is to trace our family tree. By asking ourselves who our grandparents or great-great grandparents are, we very quickly find that most peoples' backgrounds are not as straightforward as we might think. If, for example, a person decides to trace his or her ancestors at the local library or on the Internet, it can be difficult to answer questions such as: Am I black, white, or **mixed-race?** Am I American, Italian, or Indian? Am I German or Japanese? By thinking about family history, people often find that they end up describing and understanding themselves in many different ways.

❝As we are liberated from our own fear, our presence automatically liberates others.❞

Nelson Mandela in his inaugural speech as the first black president of South Africa in 1994

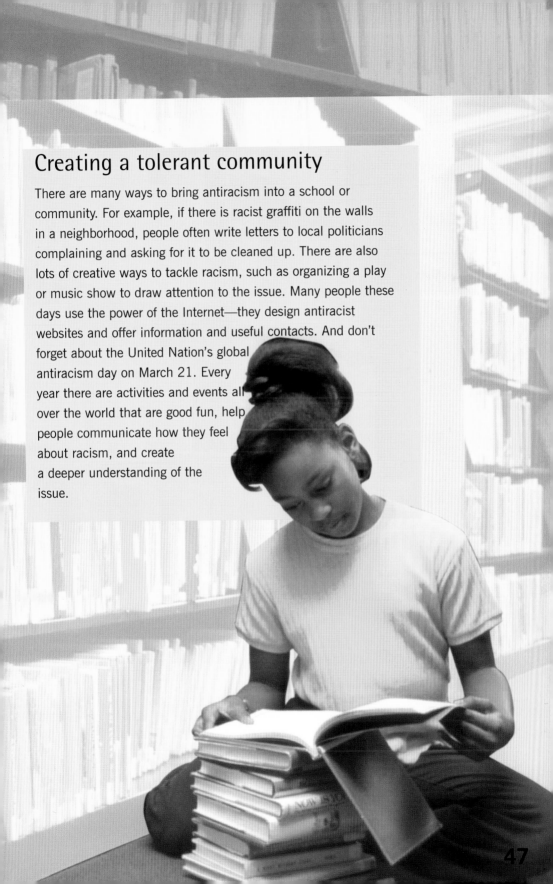

Creating a tolerant community

There are many ways to bring antiracism into a school or community. For example, if there is racist graffiti on the walls in a neighborhood, people often write letters to local politicians complaining and asking for it to be cleaned up. There are also lots of creative ways to tackle racism, such as organizing a play or music show to draw attention to the issue. Many people these days use the power of the Internet—they design antiracist websites and offer information and useful contacts. And don't forget about the United Nation's global antiracism day on March 21. Every year there are activities and events all over the world that are good fun, help people communicate how they feel about racism, and create a deeper understanding of the issue.

Experiences of Racism

If a person is physically attacked, or if his or her home, family, or friends are attacked, he or she must report the incident to the police immediately. But, as this book has shown, racism is not always physical. If any sort of racial abuse is experienced, there are many people and organizations who can listen and help. The most important thing to remember is that racism is against the law in the United States, Britain, and Europe, in fact, the world over. Though the laws vary slightly from country to country, it is everybody's right to challenge racism.

Whom should I talk to?

Racism can be difficult to talk about. But whether racism is experienced at school or in a **community,** there are always people close by who can help. One of the first things to do is write down the things that happen, noting the dates and places. This can help people express their fears, but this record may also be useful to help prove that racism has been experienced or witnessed. A teacher, a friend, or someone in your family will always be there for you to listen and give advice. The same can be said if a friend or a neighbor is experiencing racism; being there to listen and talk helps people express their frustrations or fears.

What will happen when I speak to someone?

The action and advice that people you talk to might give depends on what sort of racism you experienced. Sometimes talking to a teacher, family member, or friend won't be enough, and in these cases a more official complaint may be necessary. This may sound intimidating, but it's very important to report racial incidents so that they can be resolved. If they're not reported, racist behavior can spread and could hurt someone else.

Who else can I contact?

There are many local, national, and worldwide organizations that are dedicated to helping stop racism. If people find it difficult to talk to relatives or friends, then these organizations will provide support. It is worth looking in the local telephone book for organizations, or asking in a nearby library. There is also a list at the back of this book, suggesting people who will gladly listen, help, and offer more advice and information.

Facts and Figures

Hate crime and criminal justice

United States

• In 2000, 9,430 hate crimes were reported to law enforcement agencies across the country.

• 65 percent of these hate crimes were directed at individuals, while 34.4 percent were against property.

• 32.1 percent occurred in or around residential properties, while 17.4 percent happened on the street or on highways. Intimidation was the most frequently reported crime.

• In 1999 a report revealed that, out of 175,000 stop-and-search incidents over a 15-month period in New York, black people were 6 times more likely to be stopped by police.

• In 1999 a report in New Jersey revealed that out of all people stopped and searched by police, 77.2 percent were people of color.

Great Britain

• The British Crime Survey estimated that about 130,000 racially motivated crimes were committed against black and Asian people in 1997.

• In Britain 18 percent of male prisoners and 24 percent of female prisoners are from ethnic minorities. One-third of all young black people in Britain come into contact with the justice system by their late twenties.

• Black and ethnic minority people are 5 times more likely than white people to be stopped and searched by the police. In London only 20 percent of the population are from ethnic minority groups, but they make up 43 percent of those stopped and searched.

Australia

• The imprisonment rate for **indigenous** (Aboriginal or Torres Islander) adults in 1997 was more than 14 times that for nonindigenous adults.

• In 1996 an indigenous youth was 21 times more likely to be detained in custody than a nonindigenous youth.

• In 1998 the rate of imprisonment for indigenous males aged 20–29 was 1 in 20, compared with 1 in 200 for nonindigenous males of the same age.

Racism on the Internet

• In 1995, there was one racist website in North America, today there are more than 1,400.
• The European Union reported 2,100 hate sites, with 300 based in Germany.
• Ethnic minorities and low-income families are the least likely people in society to own a computer and use the Internet.
• 13 percent of young black people and 12.1 percent of young Latino people in the United States have access to the Internet, compared with 35.8 percent of white youth.

The rise of extremist politics in Europe

In September 2001 the **United Nations** Commission on Human Rights expressed a concern about the rise of extreme political groups: "Neo-fascism and neo-Nazism are gaining ground in many countries—especially Europe."

France —the right-wing Front Nationale won 17.9 percent of the vote during the second round of the French presidential elections in 2002.
Norway—the Progress Party, an anti-immigration party, won 14.6 percent of the 2001 general election vote.
Britain—the British National Party, a neo-Nazi party, scored 11.4 percent of the local election votes in 2002.
Italy—in 1995 the National Alliance, formerly the postwar fascist Italian Social Movement, changed its name and scored 12 percent of the votes in the 2001 general election.
Austria—in 1999, the Freedom Party, an anti-immigration, antirefugee party, scored 26.9 percent of the votes in the general election.

Further Information

Contacts

American Civil Liberties Union
125 Broad Street, 18th floor
New York, NY 10004
e-mail: aclu@aclu.org
www.aclu.org

Amnesty International
National Office
322 Eighth Avenue
New York, NY 10001
(212) 807-8400
e-mail: adminus@aiusa.org
www.amnestyusa.org

CORE (Congress of Racial Equality)
817 Broadway, 3rd Floor
New York, NY 10003
(212) 598-4000
e-mail: core@core-online.org
www.core-online.org

**NAACCP (National Association for the
Advancement of Colored People)**
4805 Mt. Hope Drive
Baltimore, MD 21215
(410) 521-4939
e-mail: washingtonbureau@naacpnet.org
www.naacp.org

Rainbow/Push Coalition
930 East 50th Street
Chicago, IL 60615
(773) 373-3366
e-mail: info@rainbowpush.org
www.rainbowpush.org

United Nations Youth Unit
2 UN Plaza, 13th Floor
New York, NY 10017
(212) 963-2791
e-mail: ilenko@un.org
www.un.org/youth

U.S. Department of Justice
950 Pennsylvania Avenue NW
Washington, DC 20530
(202) 514 3831
e-mail: AskDOJ@usdoj.gov
www.usdoj.gov

U.S. Department of State
2201 C Street NW
Washington, D.C. 20520
(202) 647-4000
e-mail: Secretary@state.gov
www.state.gov

Further reading

Cole, Michael D. *The L.A. Riots: Rage in the City of the Angels.* Berkeley Heights, N.J.: Enslow, 1999.

Finlayson, Reggie. *Nelson Mandela.* Minneapolis: Lerner, 1998.

Gay, Kathleen. *I Am Who I Am: Speaking Out About Multiracial Identity.* Danbury, Conn.: Scholastic, 2000.

Grant, Rich G. *Racism: Changing Attitudes, 1900–2000.* Chicago: Raintree, 2000.

LaMachia, John. *So What Is Tolerance Anyway?* New York: Rosen, 2000.

Levy, Debbie. *Bigotry.* Farmington Hills, Mich.: Gale Group, 2001.

Newman, Amy. *The Nuremburg Laws.* Farmington Hills, Mich.: Gale Group, 1998.

Pasco, Elaine. *Racial Prejudice: Why Can't We Overcome?* Danbury, Conn.: Scholastic, 2000.

Glossary

abolitionist individual or group of people that actively campaigns for the end of an injustice, for example, slavery

acquit free or release from a charge or a crime

anti-Semitic term describing prejudice or hostility directed toward Jewish people

apartheid government in South Africa that systematically segregated and discriminated against non-European Africans. It lasted from 1948 to 1994.

Aryan originally referred to peoples speaking a mixture of European and Indian languages. The Nazi Party, however, falsely believed that the term referred to peoples of Scandinavian descent. They twisted this idea further to describe Aryans as the "master race," which excluded Jews, Slavs, and Africans. The theory was based on a false racial theory of the 1800s.

asylum protection from arrest and persecution given by another nation, embassy, or agency

boycott form of protest involving the breaking of links (for example, with a country) or not using a business or service

civil rights legal and moral rights of people in a country

community group of people who share the same general space and interests in life

concentration camp prison camp that holds nonmilitary prisoners (civilians)

democracy political system in which a country's leaders are elected by the people

direct discrimination openly favoring or harming one group of people over another because of race, religion, nationality, or other grouping

discrimination unfair treatment of a person on the grounds that he or she belongs to a different ethnic group, religion, or other category

DNA (deoxyribonucleic acid) molecules that carry qualities, potentials, and physical characteristics from one generation to the next

dysentery infection of the intestine

ethnic group group of people who share the same national or cultural history

European Parliament part of the decision-making apparatus of the European Union, made up of representatives elected by each of the member states

European Union alliance among fifteen European countries, known as "member states"

evolution process that describes how living animals or plants change over time

fascist person who believes in an extreme set of nationalist and militarist political views

genes sequences in a biological cell that contain DNA

genetics branch of biology that studies heredity and variation in life

genocide deliberate and systematic destruction of an entire political or ethnic group

genome an organism's entire genetic makeup

ghetto originally a part of a city set aside for Jews. Today it is used loosely to mean a poor area with a majority of ethnic minority residents

homophobia prejudice against homosexual people

human rights each person's right to liberty and justice

indigenous originating from a country or region

indirect discrimination deep-rooted discrimination in which the effects of certain rules in society disadvantages a particular group or groups of people

Industrial Revolution period during the 18th and 19th centuries when first Britain and then other European countries and the United States were transformed from farming into industrial nations

integrate blend in with or cooperate with other ethnic groups in a society

"Jim Crow" laws series of laws introduced in southern states at the end of the Civil War that enforced **segregation** of African Americans from whites in public places such as schools, restaurants, theaters, and restrooms

Kosovan person or group of people from the Kosovo area within the republic of Serbia in former Yugoslavia

legislation process of making laws

migrant person who moves from a town, city, or county to settle in another

migrate move from one area or country to another

minority ethnic or other group that doesn't represent the majority in a neighborhood, town, city, or country

mixed-race from more than one racial or ethnic group. People from mixed races are the fastest growing racial group in the United States.

oppression arbitrary and cruel exercise of power over a person or group

prejudice fixed ideas about a person or group of people that aren't based on knowledge or fact

propaganda use of the media to influence people's opinions

pseudo false or fake

Roma person or ethnic group, originally from southern Asia. The term has recently come to be associated with people from Eastern Europe.

segregate separation of different ethnic groups in society, especially in housing, education, or public transportation

sexism prejudice against the opposite sex

smallpox very contagious and deadly disease. The sufferer develops a high fever and a rash of blisters.

Social Darwinism pseudo scientific theory based on the idea that ethnic groups and races are subject to the same laws of natural selection that Charles Darwin discovered in plant and animal life

species individual animals or plants that have common biological attributes

stereotype definition of a person according to his or her physical characteristics, regardless of that person's individual personality or abilities

United Nations voluntary association of countries that have joined together to promote international peace and security

xenophobia fear of the unknown or the foreign

Index